Dedication

To my babies, who finds my cussing adorable.
~Twigs

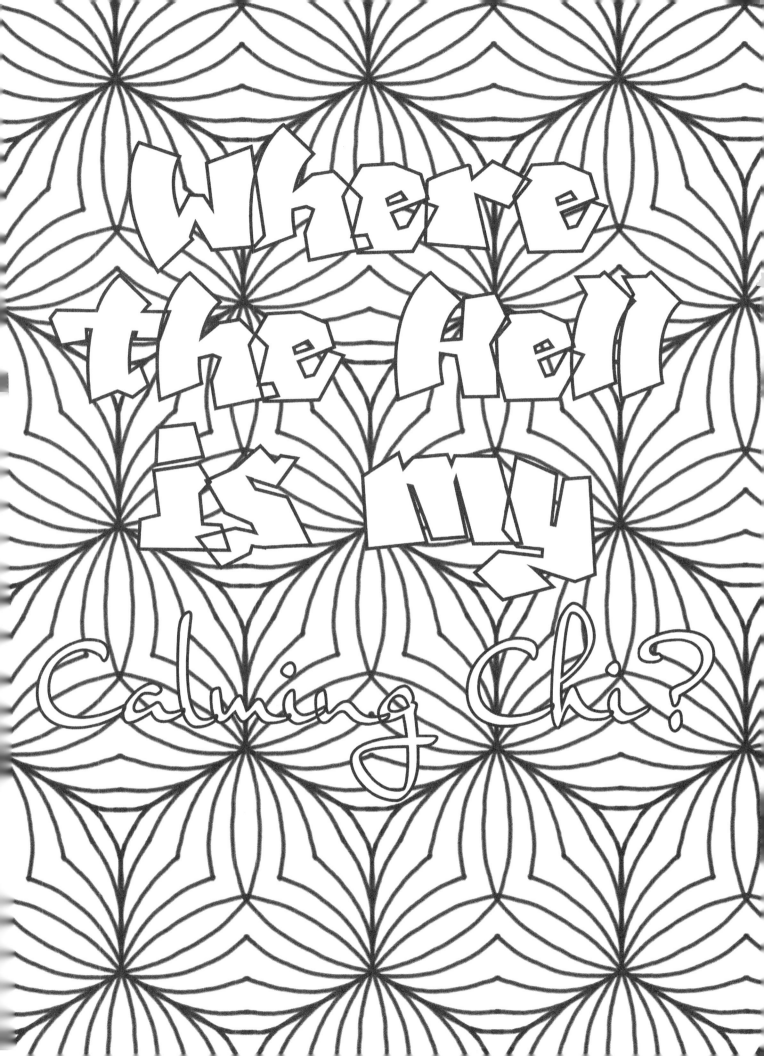

Why are there so many dumb fucking people in my life?!

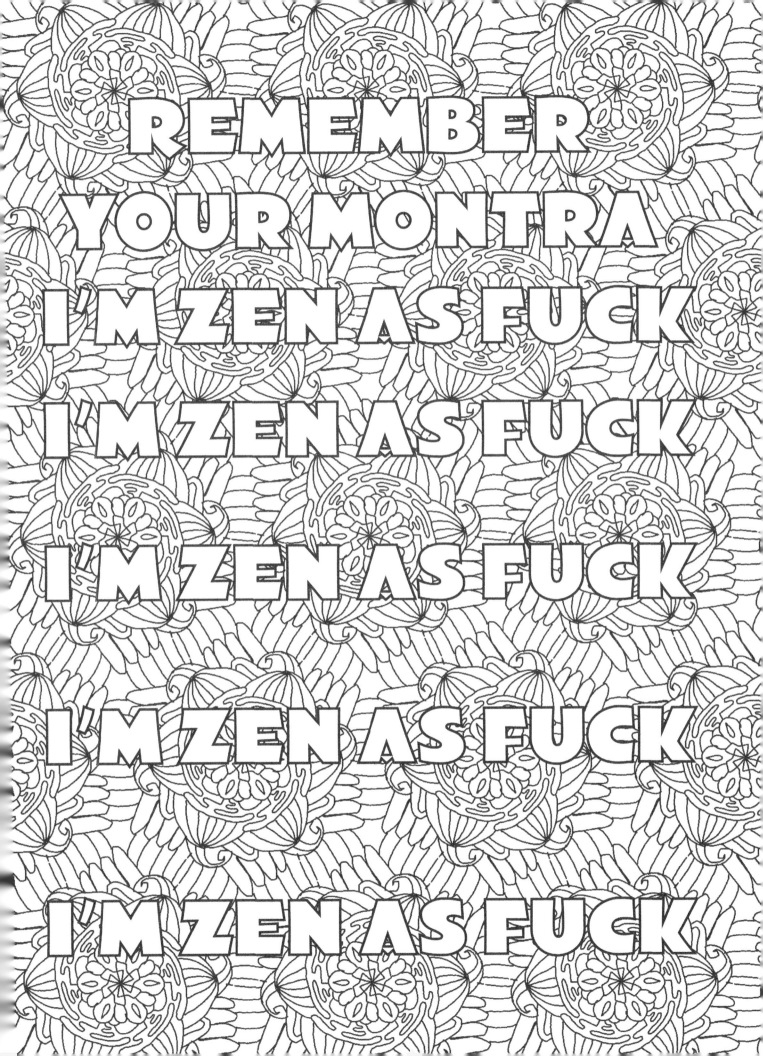

Other titles by Twigs Greenpage

<u>**Coloring books**</u>
Accessible Coloring Book
Humorous Hummingbirds Coloring Book
Scardy Pardy and Friends - Boston Terrier Coloring Book
Ellis Island Gateway to Freedom Coloring Book
The Beatz Sweets Farm Coloring Book
Nature Mandala Coloring Book
Zen as Fuck: A Cussing Coloring Book

<u>**Prompt Journals**</u>
Zen as F*ck
What's up Monkey Butt
Today We Garden
30 Day Drawing Challenge Journal
Escape Room Tracker: Scrapbook

<u>**ADHD Resources**</u>
Daily Behavior Report Card
Keep Calm and Start Doing
My ADHD Adventure
Code of Conduct

Doodle Notebooks

Dot Grid Journals

Bullet Planners

Many Blank Journals and Notebooks are available as well.

Made in the USA
Monee, IL
29 July 2022